The town is busy today.

Four small wheels go around.
What is it?

Beep! Beep!

horn

wheel

It is a blue car. It has a horn.

Ten big wheels go around.
What is it?

It is a **green** truck. It has a loud engine.

vrooooom!

engine

Two thin wheels go around.
What is it?

Ring! Ring!

It is a **white** bicycle. It has a nice bell.

Eight fat wheels go around.
What is it?

It is a yellow bus.
It has big wipers.

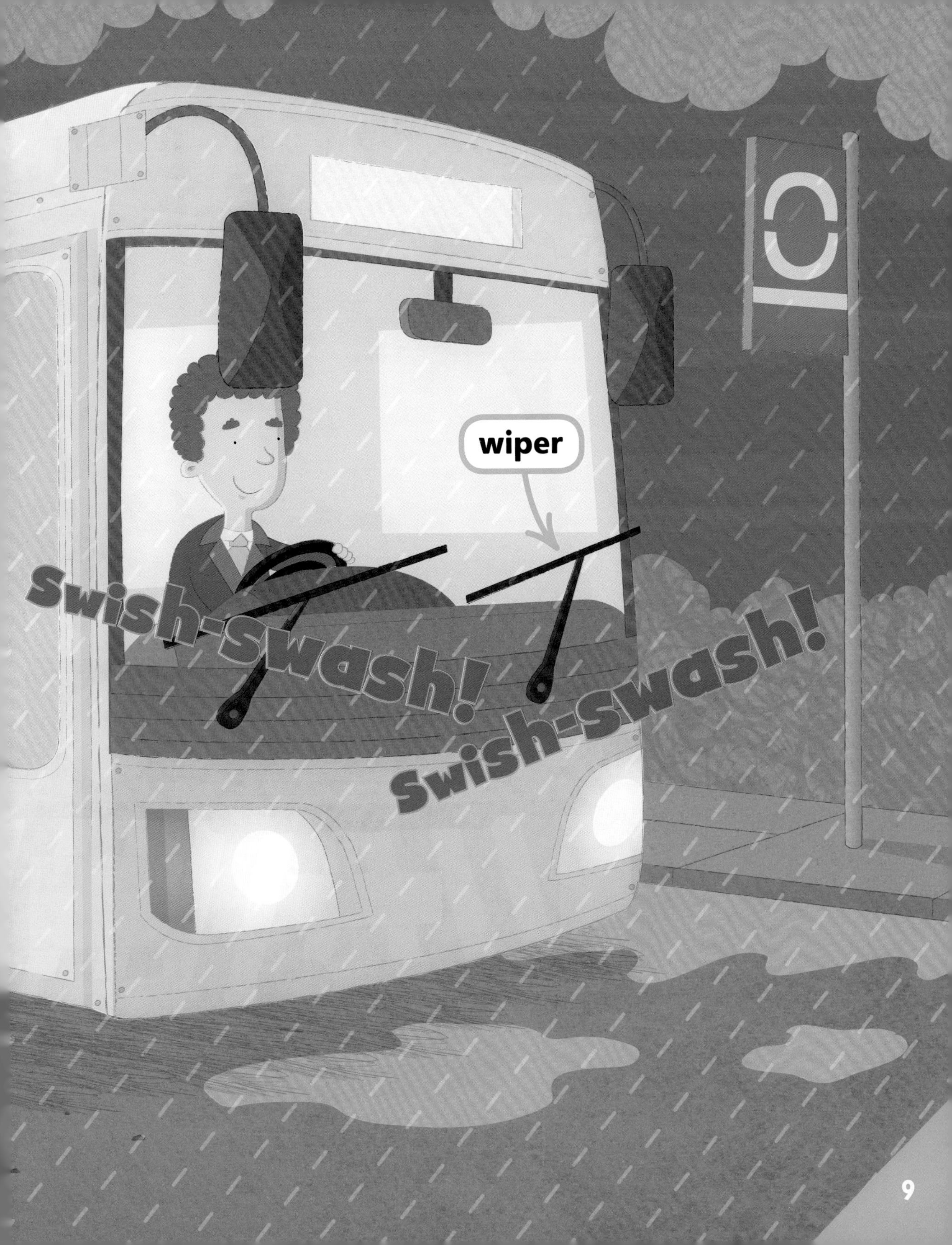
wiper
Swish-Swash!
Swish-Swash!

Twelve **black** wheels go around.
What is it?

Wooo!

Wooo!

It is a **red** fire truck.
It has a loud siren.

Six big wheels go around.
What is it?

rumble rumble

mixer

It is an **orange** cement mixer.
The mixer goes around and around.

Activities

Before You Read

1 What do you see on page 1?

After You Read

1 Read and match.

fire truck   bicycle   truck   car   cement mixer   bus

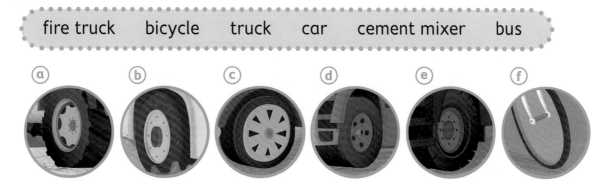

ⓐ   ⓑ   ⓒ   ⓓ   ⓔ   ⓕ

2 Read and say *Yes* or *No*.
  a A fire truck has a siren.
  b A bus has a mixer.
  c A car has a horn.
  d A bicycle has wipers.
  e A cement mixer has a bell.
  f A truck has an engine.

Pearson Education Limited
Edinburgh Gate, Harlow,
Essex CM20 2JE, England
and Associated Companies throughout the world.

ISBN: 978-1-4479-4437-9

This edition first published by Pearson Education Ltd 2013

9 10

Set in 19/23pt OT Fiendstar
Printed in Slovakia by Neografia

Acknowledgements
Illustrations: Mike Byrne (Advocate)

Published by Pearson Education Ltd

For a complete list of the titles available in the Pearson English Kids Readers series, please go to
www.pearsonenglishkidsreaders.com. Alternatively, write to your local Pearson Education office or to
Pearson English Readers Marketing Department, Pearson Education, Edinburgh Gate, Harlow, Essex CM20 2JE, England.